YOUR KNOWLEDGE HA

- We will publish your bachelor's and master's thesis, essays and papers

- Your own eBook and book - sold worldwide in all relevant shops

- Earn money with each sale

Upload your text at www.GRIN.com and publish for free

Deepak Tanwar

Comprehensive Reanalysis of Genomic Storm (Transcriptomic) Data, Integrating Clinical Varibles and Utilizing New and Old Approaches

GRIN Publishing

Bibliographic information published by the German National Library:

The German National Library lists this publication in the National Bibliography; detailed bibliographic data are available on the Internet at http://dnb.dnb.de .

Imprint:

Copyright © 2014 GRIN Verlag GmbH
Print and binding: Books on Demand GmbH, Norderstedt Germany
ISBN: 978-3-656-85845-4

This book at GRIN:

http://www.grin.com/en/e-book/284986/comprehensive-reanalysis-of-genomic-storm-transcriptomic-data-integrating

GRIN - Your knowledge has value

Since its foundation in 1998, GRIN has specialized in publishing academic texts by students, college teachers and other academics as e-book and printed book. The website www.grin.com is an ideal platform for presenting term papers, final papers, scientific essays, dissertations and specialist books.

Visit us on the internet:

http://www.grin.com/

http://www.facebook.com/grincom

http://www.twitter.com/grin_com

2014

AMITY INSTITUTE of BIOTECHNOLOGY

AMITY UNIVERSITY RAJASTHAN

B.Tech. Bioinformatics Thesis

Submitted by:

Deepak Kumar Tanwar

Amity Institute of Biotechnology

Amity University Rajasthan

Comprehensive Reanalysis of Genomic Storm (Transcriptomic) Data, Integrating Clinical Varibles and Utilizing New and Old Approaches

A thesis submitted in fulfilment of the requirements for the degree of B.Tech. Bioinformatics to Amity Institute of Biotechnology, Amity University Rajasthan, Jaipur

ACKNOWLEDGEMENTS

The main part of my work was carried out from 19th June, 2013 to 29th January, 2014 in the Network Modelling group at the **Hans-Knöll-Institut (HKI) and the Centre for Sepsis Control and Care (CSCC), University Hospital Jena, Germany.** This Bachelor of Technology Thesis is very multidisciplinary since I was dealing with one of the largest Trauma time series dataset through computational approaches.

First and foremost, I would like to thank **Prof. Dr. Rainer König** for accepting me to perform my thesis in his group. I am mostly indebted to my thesis supervisors Prof. Dr. Rainer König and **Dr. Sandro Lindig** for their great advice, support and constructive comments. I am convinced that my research will be related to Sepsis for a very long time.

I would also like to thank my parents for supporting me during most part of my studies and for giving me the values of hard work and patience. I sincerely thank to the Director of Amity Institute of Biotechnology, **Prof. Dr. A. N. Pathak**, who allowed me and supported me to perform research for a longer period of time. I would also like to thank most of my teachers from my home University (**Amity University Rajasthan**) for nurturing my curiosity and impressing me of the pleasure of knowledge.

And last but not least, I would like to express my deepest gratitude to my colleagues, Dr. Marcus Oswald, Miss. Antje Beiring and Miss. Janine Freitag who has been the source of inspiration for this B.Tech. Thesis.

I have enjoyed the friendly and encouraging atmosphere. I also had excellent working facilities at the HKI.

Jena, January, 2014.

Deepak K Tanwar.

Aim: I sought to determine trauma-specific transcriptomic signatures for septic sub-cohorts.

Methods: In retrospective large-scale data analysis, I applied (old and new methods), including lagged correlation between transcripts and clinical subtype counts (by integrating over 800 samples from trauma patients).

Results: Focussing on novel pathways and correlation methods we revealed (persistently down-regulated) ribosomal genes and changed time profiles of metabolic enzyme precursors /transcripts. Candidates associated to insulin signalling, including HK3, hinted towards "metabolic syndrome". Correlation analysis yielded robust results for LCN2 and LTF ($r > 0.9$), but only moderate associations to subtype counts (e.g. top-performing r (Eosinophil, IL5RA)>0.6).

Discussion: Gene Centred Normalisation Reduces Ambiguity and Improves Interpretation.

Contents

Contents

LIST of FIGURES

List of Figures

LIST of TABLES

1. THEORY

1.1 Normalization [1]

Normalization is the attempt to compensate for systematic technical differences between chips, to see more clearly the systematic biological differences between samples. Differences in treatment of two samples, especially in labelling and in hybridization, bias the relative measures on any two chips.

Systematic non-biological differences between chips are evident in several ways:

- Total brightness differs between chips
- One dye seems stronger than the other (in 2-color systems) on one chip, but not on another
- Typical background is higher in one chip than on another

There are also many non–obvious systematic differences between chips in an experiment, and even between the two channels on a single array. Some causes of systematic measurement variation include:

- Different amounts of RNA
- One dye is more readily incorporated than the other (in 2-color systems)
- The hybridisation reaction may proceed more fully to equilibrium in one array than the other
- Hybridisation conditions may vary across an array
- Scanner settings are often different, and of course
- Murphy's Law predicts even more variation than can be simply explained.

1.2 Comparison of two group of samples [2]

The simplest and most common experimental set-up is to compare two groups: for example, Treatment vs. Control, or Mutant vs. Wild type. The issues arising in simple comparisons arise also in more complex settings; it is easier to explain these in the simpler context. The long-time standard test statistic for comparing two groups is the t-statistic:

$$t = (x_{i,1} - x_{i,2}) / s_i,$$

Where $x_{i,1}$ is the mean value of gene i in group 1, $x_{i,2}$ is the mean in group 2, and s_i is the (non-pooled) within-groups standard error (SE) for gene i.

1.3 Signal Log Ratio Algorithm [3]

Signal Log Ratio algorithm estimates the measure and the direction of change of a Gene/transcript when two arrays are compared. Each probe pair on the experiment array is compared to the corresponding probe pair in the baseline arrays in the calculation of Signal Log Ratio. This process eliminates differences due to different probe binding coefficients. A One-Step Tukey's Biweight method is used in computing the Signal Log Ratio value by taking a mean of the log ratios of probe pair intensities across the two arrays. The base 2 log scale is used, translating the Signal Log Ratio of 1.0 to a 2-fold increase in the expression level and of -1.0 to a 2-fold decrease. No change in the expression level is thus indicated by a Signal Log Ratio value 0. Tukey's Biweight method also gives estimate of the amount of variation in the data. Confidence intervals are generated from the scale of variation of the data. A 95% confidence interval shows a range of values, which will include the true value 95% of the time. Small confidence interval implies that the expression data is more exact, while large confidence intervals reflect more noise and uncertainty in estimating the true level. Since the confidence intervals attached to Signal Log Ratios are computed from variation between probes, they may not reflect the full width of experimental variation.

1.4 Correlation (r) [3]

The correlation of two variables represents the degree to which the variables are related. When two variables are perfectly linearly related, the points in the scatter plot fall on a straight line. Correlation measures only linear relationship. Two summary measures or correlation coefficients, Pearson's correlation and Spearman's rho, are most commonly used. Both of these measure range from perfectly positive linear relationship to perfectly negative linear relationship, or from -1 to 1. It is not wrong to calculate the correlation between variables, which are not linearly related, but it does not make much sense. If the variables are not linearly related, the correlation does not describe their relationships effectively, and no conclusions can be based on the correlation coefficient only. Correlation and scatter plot are a good example of how numerical and graphical tools effectively complement each other.

1.5 Log2-transformation [3]

Log2-transformation is often used with DNA microarray experiments. Usually, the intensity ratio is log2-transformed. The resulting new variable is called log ratio. The increase of one in the log ratio means that the actual intensity or expression has doubled.

1.6 Intensity ratio [3]

The simplest approach is to divide the intensity of a gene in the sample by the intensity level of the same gene in the control.

1.7 Hypothesis pair [3]

Before applying the test to the data, a hypothesis pair should be formed. A hypothesis pair consists of a null hypothesis (H0) and an alternative hypothesis (H1). For the tests, the hypotheses are always formulated as follows:

H0=> There is no difference in means between compared groups

H1=> There is a difference in means between compared groups.

1.8 Threshold for p-value [3]

The p-value is usually associated with a statistical test, and it is the risk that we reject the null hypothesis, when it actually is true. Before testing, a threshold for p-value should be decided. This is a cut-off below which the results are statistically significant, and above which the results are not statistically significant. Often a threshold of 0.05 is used. This means that every 20th time we conclude by chance alone that the difference between groups is statistically signif-icant, when it actually isn't. If the compared groups are large enough, even the tiniest difference can get a significant p-value. In such cases it needs to be carefully weighted whether the statistical significance is just that, statistical significance, or is there real biological phenomenon acting in the background.

1.9 Fold change [3]

Another means to make the distribution of intensity ratios more symmetrical is to calculate the fold change. The fold change is equal to the intensity ratio, when the expression is higher than one. Below one, the fold change is equal to the inversed intensity ratio.

$$\text{For values} > 1, \text{ fold change} = \frac{Cy3'}{Cy5'}$$
$$\text{For values} < 1, \text{ fold change} = \frac{1}{(Cy3'/Cy5')}$$

The fold change makes the distribution of the expression values more sym-metric, and both under and over-expressed genes can take values between zero and infinity. Note, that the fold change makes the expression values additive in a similar fashion as the log-transformation.

1.10   Time series [3]

In a time series experiment expression changes are monitored with samples taken between certain time intervals. Although several replicates can be made per every time point, it should be considered that these replicate chips can possible be made a better use of, if they are added to the time series as sampling points. That is, it should be weighted whether a high precision in every time point is more valuable than the additional information of expression changes new sampling points (time points) produce.

1.11   Microarray preparation [4]

Microarrays are commonly prepared on a glass, nylon or quartz substrate. Critical steps in this process include the selection and nature of the DNA sequences that will be placed on the array, and the technique of fixing the sequences on the substrate. Affymetrix Company that is a leading manufacturer of gene chips, uses a method adopted from the semiconductor industry with photolithography and combinatorial chemistry. The density of oligonucleotides in their GeneChips is reported as about half a million sequences per 1.282 cm^2.(Affymetrix web site).

1.12   Probe preparation, hybridization and imaging [4]

To prepare RNA probes fro reacting with the microarray, the first step is isolation of the RNA population from the experimental and control samples. cDNA copies of the mRNAs are synthesized using reverse transcriptase and then by in vitro transcription cDNA is converted to cRNA and fluorescently labeled. This probe mixture is then cast onto the microarray. RNAs that are complementary to the molecules on the microarray hybridize with the strands on the microarray. After hybridization and probe washing the microarray substrate is visualized using the appropriate method based on the nature of substrate. With high density chips this generally requires verysensitive microscopic scanning of the chip. Oligonucleotide spots that hybridize with the RNA will show a signal based on the level of the labeled RNA that hybridized to the specific sequence. Whereas the dark spots that show little or no signal, mark sequences that are not represented in the population of expressed mRNAs.

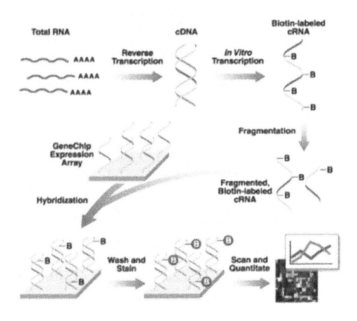

FIG. 1: The process of fluorescently labeled RNA probe production (From Affymetrix website).

1.13   Low level information analysis [4]

Microarrays measure the target quantity (i.e. relative or absolute mRNA abundance) indirectly by measuring another physical quantity – the intensity of the fluorescence of the spots on the array for each fluorescent dye. These images should be later transformed into the gene expression matrix. This task is not a trivial one because:

1. The spots corresponding to genes should be identified.

2. The boundaries of the spots should be determined.

3. The fluorescence intensity should be determined depending on the background intensity.

FIG.2 : Gene expression data. Each spot represents the expression level of a gene in two different experiments. Yellow or red spots indicate that the gene is expressed in one experiment. Green spots show that the gene is expressed at same levels in both experiments.

In conclusion, microarray-based gene expression measurements are still far from giving estimates of mRNA counts per cell in the sample. The samples are relative by nature. In addition, appropriate normalization should be applied to enable gene or samples comparisons. It is important to note that even if we had the most precise tools to measure mRNA abundance in the cell; it still wouldn't provide us a full and exact picture about the cell activity because of post-translational changes.

2. INTRODUCTION

Despite continuing advances in intensive care medicine, severe sepsis and septic shock are currently among the most common causes of morbidity and mortality in intensive care. Moreover, the incidence of severe sepsis and septic shock has increased with ageing of the population over the past decade [5, 6, 7]. According to the University Hospital Jena Website: in Germany, 154,000 new cases of Sepsis occurs every year, killing an average of 150 patients every day. Therefore, Sepsis is regarded as a hidden healthcare disaster [8]

2.1 SIRS, Sepsis and Septic Shock

For many years' doctors, attending intensive care units used a variety of terms to describe illnesses associated with infection, or illness that looked like infection. These terms included sepsis, septicaemia, bacteraemia, infection, septic shock, toxic shock etc. Unfortunately there were two problems with these terms: 1. there were no strict definitions for the terms used, and often these words or phrases were used incorrectly. 2, an emerging body of evidence arose which led us to believe that systemic inflammation, rather than infection, was responsible for multi-organ failure [9]. In the early 1990s a consensus conference between the ACCP and the SCCM laid out a new series of definitions [10]:

- **Infection**

A host response to the presence of microorganism or tissue invasion by microorganisms.

- **Bacteraemia.**

The presence of viable bacteria in circulating blood

- **Systemic Inflammatory Response Syndrome (SIRS)**

The systemic inflammatory response to a wide variety of severe clinical insults, manifested by two or more of the following conditions:

Temperature > 38°C or < 36°C

Heart rate > 90 beats/min

Respiratory rate > 20 breaths/min or $PaCO_2$ < 32 mm Hg

WBC count > 12,000/mm^3 , < 4000/mm^3 , or > 10% immature (band) forms.

Introduction

- **Sepsis**

The systemic inflammatory response to infection. In association with infection, manifestations of sepsis are the same as those previously defined for SIRS. It should be determined whether they are a direct systemic response to the presence of an infectious process and represent an acute alteration from baseline in the absence of other known causes for such abnormalities. The clinical manifestations would include two or more of the following conditions as a result of a documented infection:

- **Severe Sepsis/SIRS.**

Sepsis (SIRS) associated with organ dysfunction, hypoperfusion, or hypotension. Hypoperfusion and perfusion abnormalities may include, but are not limited to, lactic acidosis, oliguria, or an acute alteration in mental status.

- **Refractory (Septic) Shock/SIRS Shock.**

A subset of severe sepsis (SIRS) and defined as sepsis (SIRS) induced hypotension despite adequate fluid resuscitation along with the presence of perfusion abnormalities that may include, but are not limited to, lactic acidosis, oliguria, or an acute alteration in mental status. Patients receiving inotropic or vasopressor agents may no longer be hypotensive by the time they manifest hypoperfusion abnormalities or organ dysfunction, yet they would still be considered to have septic (SIRS) shock.

- **Multiple Organ Dysfunction Syndrome (MODS).**

Presence of altered organ function in an acutely ill patient such that homeostasis cannot be maintained without intervention

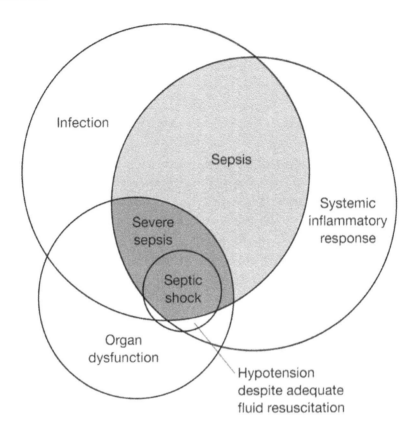

FIG.3 : Relationship of Infection, SIRS, Sepsis, Severe Sepsis and Septic Shock [11]

2.2 Related Background

Trauma represents a frequent clinical syndrome characterized by the patient's systemic inflammatory response to infection, and carries a very high mortality rate. Trauma injuries frequently lead to infections, sepsis, and multiple organ failure (MOF) [12, 13], which contribute to 51%–61% of late trauma mortality [14]. Traumatic injury with its potential for infection was likely a common cause of death for our human ancestors. Even today, massive injury remains the most common cause of death for those under the age of 45 yr in developed countries [15, 16]. Systematic screening approaches are necessary in order to better diagnose and treat trauma, because it's a complex disease state with time-dependent intra-patient variability [17]. A number of clinical trials for treating late trauma complications have failed, believed partly due to the inability to identify a proper patient population as well as the limited understanding of the interplay of biological processes underlying post-injury inflammatory complications [18, 19].

Furthermore, potential influential factors in sepsis, including treatment, age, sex and organ failure as well as interactions among these factors are assumed to play a major role in disease progression and are potentially reflected in molecular markers. Only recently has the human injury response been studied systematically at the genomic level and only now is it beginning to become better understood. Prior work has focused on the role of individual mediators [20,21,22] or processes such as apoptosis and cellular death in nosocomial infections and organ injury after trauma [23]. Circulating blood leukocytes have the capacity to seek out, recognise, and mount an appropriate inflammatory response at the earliest sign of injury. Blood neutrophils, monocytes, and Natural Killer cells are implicated as primary effectors during the initial inflammation and activation of innate immunity. Severe trauma has also been characterised by immunosuppression, primarily seen on the adaptive immune system with T lymphocyte populations being the most markedly affected cell population [24,25].

2.3 .CEL File Description

The CEL file stores the results of the intensity calculations on the pixel values of the DAT file (Contains the pixel intensity values collected from an Affymetrix Scanner). This includes an intensity value, standard deviation of the intensity, the number of pixels used to calculate the intensity value, a flag to indicate an outlier as calculated by the algorithm and a user defined flag indicating the feature should be excluded from future analysis. The file stores the previously stated data for each feature on the probe array [26].

2.4 Gene Expression Omnibus (GEO)

GEO is an international public repository that archives and freely distributes microarray, next-generation sequencing, and other forms of high-throughput functional genomics data submitted by the research community [27].

2.5 KEGG

Kyoto Encyclopaedia of Genes and Genomes; or K.E.G.G., as it is commonly called; is a collection of online databases dealing with genomes, enzymatic pathways, and biological chemicals. The Pathway Database, records networks of molecular interactions in cells and their variants (specific to particular organisms). K.E.G.G. switched to a subscription model, accessible via FTP in July, 2011. KEGG is a database resource for understanding high-level functions and utilities of the biological system, such as the cell, the organism and the ecosystem, from genomic and molecular-level information [28].

The Kyoto Encyclopaedia of Genes and Genomes was initiated by the Japanese human genome program in 1995 [29]. According to the developers, KEGG is a "computer representation" of the biological system [30]. The KEGG database can be utilized for modelling and simulation, browsing and retrieval of data. It is a part of the systems biology approach.

KEGG is best known for the display of biochemical pathways, but many other functions are now available at KEGG. KEGG is a collection of about 20 databases, which can be divided into three groups covering different biological spaces:

- Genes
    - KEGG Genes - manually curated from completely sequenced genomes
    - DGENES - draft genomes
    - EGENES - from EST contigs
    - KEGG Orthology - manually defined ortholog groups based on KEGG pathways and BRITE functional hierarchies
    - KEGG SSDB - Seq similarity scores

- Chemicals and Ligands
    - Ligand
- Systems
    - KEGG Pathway
    - KEGG Brite

3. MATERIALS & METHODS

3.1 Data

Publicly available data sets containing gene expression values from blood samples of 167 patients between the ages of 18 and 55 yr, trauma patients (incl. septic and non-septic patients) as well as healthy controls from published studies were retrieved from Gene Expression Omnibus (GEO) [31]. Total blood leukocytes were isolated according to protocols previously published. Total cellular RNA was extracted and hybridised onto an HU133 Plus 2.0 GeneChip (Affymetrix) according to the manufacturer's recommendations. Sepsis and control samples from the Illumina platform available under GSE36809.

3.2 Data Analysis

Briefly, computations were performed using R software (http://www.r-project.org/) v.3.0.2 and Bioconductor [32] packages. To assure comparability due to differences in sample size in Sepsis patients and controls data, a consistent work-flow was applied.

Data was obtained from GEO [33] and were pre-processed using chip definition file from Brainarray (v.17, 2013), which aggregates probes into updated gene-centred probe set definitions mapping to Entrez IDs [34]. Further pre-processing was performed using quantile normalisation via the RMA method for each sample set and after merging. Differentially expressed genes (DEGs) in the data were filtered according to microarray quality control (MAQC) [35] criteria and standard thresholds as follows: (i) average two-fold difference for pooled groups (sepsis versus non-septic controls); and (ii) false discovery rate (FDR) (Benjamini–Hochberg)-adjusted P-values <0.05 from Wilcoxon test. Illumina data were converted using median averaged signals for technical bead type replicates and re-normalised after merging with Affymetrix data.

3.3 Clustering

Clustering is the task of grouping a set of objects in such a way that objects in the same group are more similar (in some sense or another) to each other than to those in other groups. Clustering was performed using the ape (Analyses of Phylogenetics and Evolution) package. Ape [36] provides functions for reading and manipulating phylogenetic trees and DNA sequences, computing DNA distances, estimating trees with distance-based methods, and a range of methods for comparative analyses and analysis of diversification. All clustering analyses were performed with agglomerative hierarchical clustering using average linkage. In order to examine the correlation between the cell lines 1− Pearson correlation was used as distance measure.

3.4 Enrichment tests

To investigate Sepsis relevant pathways in contrast to the other control samples enrichment tests were used. The test methods either need p-values or t-statistics as an input. Because of multiple hypotheses testing the p-values were Benjamini-Hochberg corrected to control the false discovery rate (*Benjamini & Hochberg, 1995*). The genes were ranked based on their corrected p-value in an ascending order and assigned to pathways using the KEGG database to create gene sets. Mapping of genes to pathways compiled 186 gene sets.

Quantitative Set Analysis for Gene Expression was performed using qusage package [37]. The qusage package accounts for inter-gene correlations using a Variance Inflation Factor technique that extends the method proposed by *Wu et al. (Nucleic Acids Res, 2012)*. In addition, rather than simply evaluating the deviation from a null hypothesis with a single number (a P value), qusage quantifies gene set activity with a complete probability density function (PDF). From this PDF, P values and confidence intervals can be easily extracted [37].

3.5 Lagged Correlation

Lagged relationships are characteristic of many natural physical systems. Lagged correlation refers to the correlation between two time series shifted in time relative to one another. Lagged correlation is important in studying the relationship between time series for two reasons. First, one series may have a delayed response to the other series, or perhaps a delayed response to a common stimulus that affects both series. Second, the response of one series to the other series or an outside stimulus may be "smeared" in time, such that a stimulus restricted to one observation elicits a response at multiple observations. For example, because of storage in reservoirs, glaciers, etc., the volume discharge of a river in one year may depend on precipitation in the several preceding years. Or because of changes in crown density and photosynthate storage, the width of a tree-ring in one year may depend on climate of several preceding years. The simple correlation coefficient between the two series properly aligned in time is inadequate to characterize the relationship in such situations. Useful functions we will examine as alternative to the simple correlation coefficient are the cross-correlation function and the impulse response function. The cross-correlation function is the correlation between the series shifted against one another as a function of number of observations of the offset. If the individual series are autocorrelated, the estimated cross-correlation function may be distorted and misleading as a measure of the lagged relationship [38].

The cross-correlation function (ccf) of two time series is the product-moment correlation as a function of lag, or time-offset, between the series. It is helpful to begin defining the ccf with a definition of the cross-covariance function (ccvf). Consider N pairs of observations on two time series, u_t and y_t. The sample ccvf is given by [38]:

$$c_{uy}(k) = \frac{1}{N} \sum_{t=1}^{N-k} (u_t - \bar{u})(y_{t+k} - \bar{y}) \qquad [k = 0, 1, \cdots, (N-1)]$$

$$c_{uy}(k) = \frac{1}{N} \sum_{t=1-k}^{N} (u_t - \bar{u})(y_{t+k} - \bar{y}) \qquad [k = -1, -2, \cdots, -(N-1)]$$

(1)

Where N is the series length, $\bar{u}$ and $\bar{y}$ is the sample means, and k is the lag. The sample cross-correlation function (ccf) is the ccvf scaled by the variances of the two series [38]:

$$r_{uy}(k) = \frac{c_{uy}(k)}{\sqrt{c_{uu}(0)c_{yy}(0)}}$$

(2)

Where, $c_{uu}(0)$ and $c_{yy}(0)$ are the sample variances of u_t and y_t.

NOTE: value at lag k equals value at lag $-k$.

The ccvf and ccf are asymmetrical functions. The asymmetry brings about the need for the two parts of equation (1). The cross-correlation function as described by equation (1) can be described in terms of "lead" and "lag" relationships. The first part of the equation applies to y_t shift forward relative to u_t. [37]

I performed lagged correlation between transcripts and clinical subtype counts to check the lagged time effects on LCN2 and HLA-DMB transcripts for Neutrophils and Lymphocytes.

3.6 Additional Information

A supplemental web-based portal (Massachusetts General Hospital, 2011) is available to explore in greater detail the largest clinical and genomic database to date from severely injured humans. Data in this study have been deposited in the GEO DataSets site under accession number GSE11375.

4. RESULTS

4.1 Differentially Expressed Genes

After pre-processing the list narrowed down to 18960 gene-centred and annotated features mapped by Entrez IDs. Filtering DEGs by FDR-adjusted P-values <0.05 (Wilcoxon test & T-Test) and average two-fold expression change yielded 1558 features for all pooled samples (septic versus non-septic groups). Because of multiple hypotheses testing the p-values were Benjamini-Hochberg corrected to control the false discovery rate (*Benjamini & Hochberg, 1995*).

TABLE 1: No. of Differentially Expressed Genes

Methods	DEGs	DEGs after FDR Correction
T-Test	13878	13673
Wilcoxon Test	14026	13787
Log2 Fold Change	1598	NA

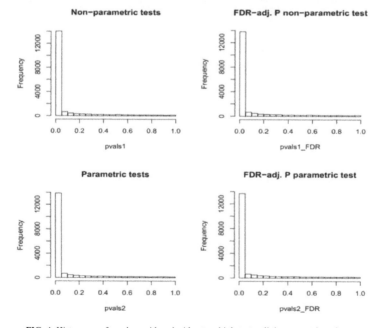

FIG. 4: Histograms of p-values with and without multiple tests adj. in parametric and non-parametric version

Results

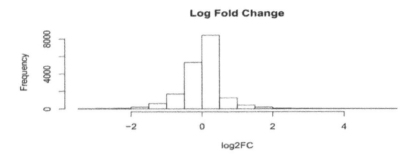

Log Fold Change

FIG. 5: Histograms of Log2 Fold Change

4.2 Clustering:

I perform the gender specific clustering taking in consideration the various time points of the patient's data. Red colour represents Females and Blue colour represents Males. It is depicted from the outcome (figure) that Controls were grouped together with gender specificity and also the samples taken at early time point were grouped together (easily seen from the pinned out part of the dendogram).

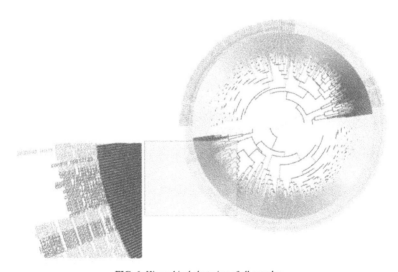

FIG. 6: Hierarchical clustering of all samples

4.3 Regulation of some important genes:

I noticed some important genes that were highly up-regulated or down-regulated in the data.

4.3.1   HLA-DMB & LCN2

HLA-DMB belongs to the HLA (Human Leukocyte Antigen) class II beta chain paralogues. This class II molecule is a heterodimer consisting of an alpha (DMA) and a beta (DMB) chain, both anchored in the membrane. DM plays a central role in the peptide loading of MHC class II molecules by helping to release the CLIP (class II-associated invariant chain peptide) molecule from the peptide binding site. Class II molecules are expressed in antigen presenting cells (APC: B lymphocytes, dendritic cells, macrophages). [39]

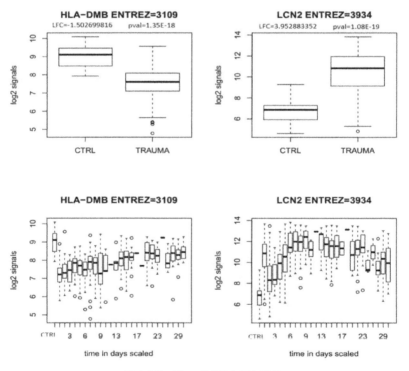

FIG. 7: Box Plots of LCN2 & HLA-DMB

Results

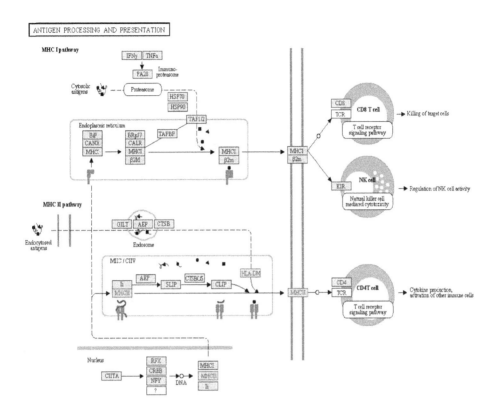

FIG. 8: Antigen Processing and Presentation Pathway [41]

T-Cells are a subset of lymphocytes that play a large role in the immune response. The TCR (T-Cell Receptor) is a complex of integral membrane proteins that participates in the activation of T-Cells in response to the presentation of antigen. Stimulation of TCR is triggered by MHC (Major Histocompatibility Complex) molecules on Antigen Presenting Cells that present antigen peptides to TCR complexes and induce a series of intracellular signaling cascades. Engagement of the TCR initiates positive (signal-enhancing) and negative (signal-attenuating) cascades that ultimately result in cellular proliferation, differentiation, Cytokine production, and/or activation-induced cell death. These signaling cascades regulate T-Cell development, homeostasis, activation, acquisition of effectors' functions and apoptosis. [40]

LCN2 (Lipocalin-2) also known as oncogene 24p3 or Neutrophil Gelatinase-Associated Lipocalin (NGAL). LCN2 is an iron-trafficking protein involved in multiple processes such as apoptosis, innate immunity and renal development. The binding of NGAL to bacterial siderophores is important in the innate immune response to bacterial infection. Upon encountering invading bacteria the toll-like receptors on immune cells stimulate the synthesis and secretion of NGAL. Secreted NGAL then limits bacterial growth by sequestering iron-containing siderophores. LCN2 also functions as growth factor. Originally, NGAL was isolated from a supernatant of activated human neutrophils.[42] Lack of LCN2 expression has been possibly linked to acne could be caused due to lack of gene expression, which possibly can be correct with Isotretinoin.[43,44].

4.3.2 Correlation of LCN 2and LTF

Lipocalin-2 (LCN2) and Lactotransferrin (LTF) found to be highly and positively correlated with the Pearson's product-moment correlation value of 0.944.

Lactoferrin (LF), also known as lactotransferrin (LTF), is a multifunctional protein of the transferrin family. Lactoferrin is a globular glycoprotein with a molecular mass of about 80 kDa that is widely represented in various secretory fluids, such as milk, saliva, tears, and nasal secretions. Lactoferrin is one of the components of the immune system of the body; it has antimicrobial activity (bacteriocide, fungicide) and is part of the innate defense, mainly at mucoses [45]. The important role of lactoferrin in human host defense and especially in lung [46]. Lactotransferrin is a major iron-binding and multifunctional protein found in exocrine fluids such as breast milk and mucosal secretions. Antimicrobial properties include bacteriostasis, which is related to its ability to sequester free iron and thus inhibit microbial growth, as well as direct bactericidal properties leading to the release of lipopolysaccharides from the bacterial outer membrane.

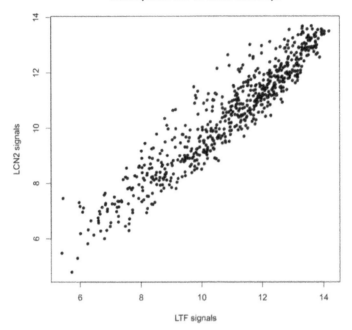

FIG. 9: Pearson's product-moment correlation of LCN2 and LTF (r = 0.9441)

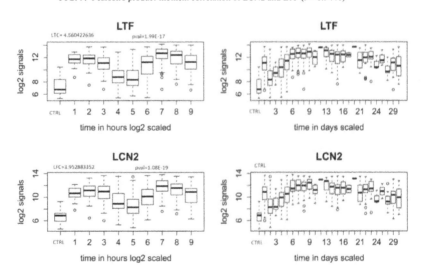

FIG. 10: LTF & LCN expression

4.3.3 SLC4A1 & IL5RA

Both the genes have shown up regulation at the later stages in patients. IL5RA was first down regulated in patients, but at later stage, it regulated positively. IL5RA was found to be highly correlating with Eosinophils ($r= 0.6136$). SLC4A1 gene did not show much effect during initial stages, but was highly up regulated in patients at last stages.

The official name of **SLC4A1** gene is "solute carrier family 4 (anion exchanger), member 1 (Diego blood group)." From NCBI Gene: [47] The protein encoded by this gene is part of the anion exchanger (AE) family and is expressed in the erythrocyte plasma membrane, where it functions as a chloride/bicarbonate exchanger involved in carbon dioxide transport from tissues to lungs. From UniProt:[48] Band 3 is the major integral glycoprotein of the erythrocyte membrane. Band 3 has two functional domains. Its integral domain mediates a 1:1 exchange of inorganic anions across the membrane, whereas its cytoplasmic domain provides binding sites for cytoskeletal proteins, glycolytic enzymes, and hemoglobin.

IL5RA Gene: The protein encoded by IL5RA (interleukin 5 receptor, alpha) gene is an interleukin 5 specific subunit of a heterodimeric cytokine receptor. Diseases associated with IL5RA include *eosinophilic esophagitis* (an allergic inflammatory condition of the esophagus, and also called allergic oesophagitis [49]. Symptoms are swallowing difficulty, food impaction, and heartburn) [50] and among its related super-pathways are *STAT3 Pathway* and *Interleukin receptor SHC signaling*. GO annotations related to this gene include *protein binding* and *interleukin-5 receptor activity*.

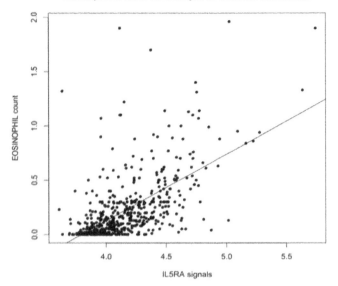

FIG. 11: Scatter plot showing Correlation of IL5RA with Eosinophils (r= 0.6136)

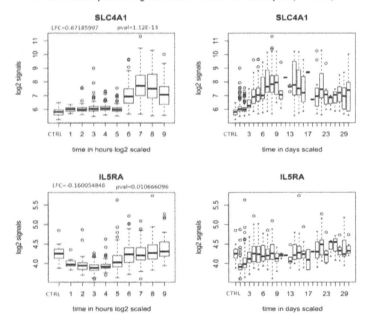

FIG. 12: Plots of IL5RA and SLC4A1

4.4 Gender Linked Genes:

DDX3Y

DX3Y (DEAD (Asp-Glu-Ala-Asp) box helicase 3, Y-linked) is a protein-coding gene and characterized by the conserved motif Asp-Glu-Ala-Asp (DEAD), are putative RNA helicases. This gene has a homolog on the X chromosome (DDX3X). The gene mutation causes male infertility, Sertoli cell only syndrome or severe hypo-spermatogenesis, suggesting that this gene plays a key role in the spermatogenic process [51] [52]. Diseases associated with DDX3Y include spermatocytoma and infertility.

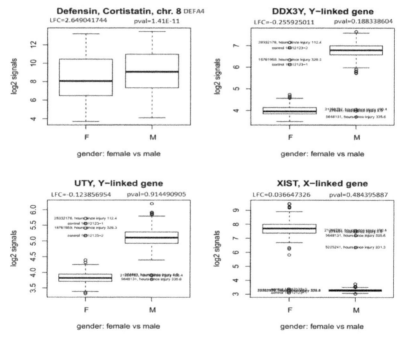

FIG. 13: Sex linked genes (outliers identified)

Results

4.5 Gene Set Enrichment Analysis (GSEA)

GSEA was performed by the qusage (Quantitative set analysis for gene expression) package. GSEA was performed to determine whether a priori defined set of genes shows statistically significant, concordant differences between two biological states. I obtained following top regulated pathways, on the basis of log fold change:

Table 2: Top KEGG pathways Enriched

Activity	Log Fold Change	Knowledgebase	Category	FDR-adj. P-value
Up regulated	0.4514927	KEGG	Folate Biosynthesis (hsa00790)	0.000000e+00
Up regulated	0.4231749	KEGG	Pathogen Escherichia Coli Infection (hsa05130)	0.000000e+00
Up regulated	0.3830689	KEGG	FC Gamma R Mediated Phagocytosis (hsa04666)	0.000000e+00
Up regulated	0.3755925	KEGG	Leukocyte Transendothelial Migration (hsa04670)	0.000000e+00
Up regulated	0.3552252	KEGG	Galactose Metabolism (hsa00052)	0.000000e+00
Up regulated	0.1783564	KEGG	Glycolysis gluconeogenesis (hsa00010)	0.000000e+00
Down regulated	-0.5441087	KEGG	Ribosome (hsa03010)	2.284539e-13
Down regulated	-0.4133383	KEGG	Primary Immunodeficiency (hsa05340)	0.000000e+00
Down regulated	-0.3768175	KEGG	Valine, Leucine and Isoleucine Biosynthesis (hsa00290)	0.000000e+00
Down regulated	-0.3728089	KEGG	Aminocyl tRNA Biosynthesis (hsa00970)	0.000000e+00
Down regulated	-0.3619649	KEGG	Graft versus Host Disease (hsa05332)	3.689376e-12

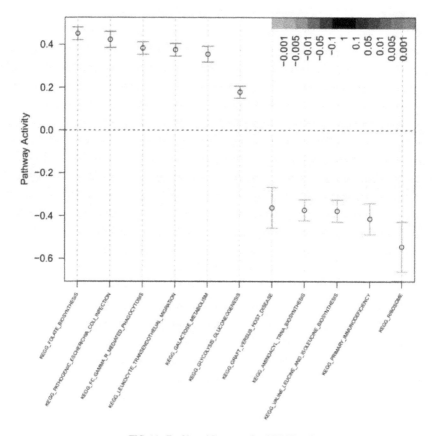

FIG. 14: Top Up and Down regulated KEGG pathways

4.5.1 Kegg Mapper

I used the KEGG Mapper (http://www.genome.jp/kegg/tool/map_pathway2.html) to construct the pathways with colour codes, displaying the genes and their positions in the pathway. I made the colour code as follows:

- Up regulated genes- RED
- Not much regulated genes- PINK
- Down regulated genes- BLUE

4.5.2 Glycolysis Gluconeogenesis

Glycolysis is the process of converting glucose into pyruvate and generating small amounts of ATP (energy) and NADH (reducing power). It is a central pathway that produces important precursor metabolites: six-carbon compounds of glucose-6P and fructose-6P and three-carbon compounds of glycerone-P, glyceraldehyde-3P, glycerate-3P, phosphoenolpyruvate, and pyruvate. Acetyl-CoA, another important precursor metabolite, is produced by oxidative decarboxylation of pyruvate. Gluconeogenesis is a synthesis pathway of glucose from non-carbohydrate precursors. It is essentially a reversal of glycolysis with minor variations of alternative paths [MD:M00003]. This pathway is the most important pathway, as it produces energy, which is required by the cells, in order to function. Septic patients have this metabolic pathway up-regulated, as the rate of metabolism increases in the patients [53].

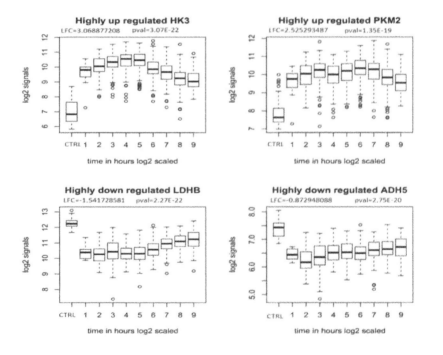

FIG. 15: Box plot of highly up and down regulated genes of Glycolysis pathway

Results

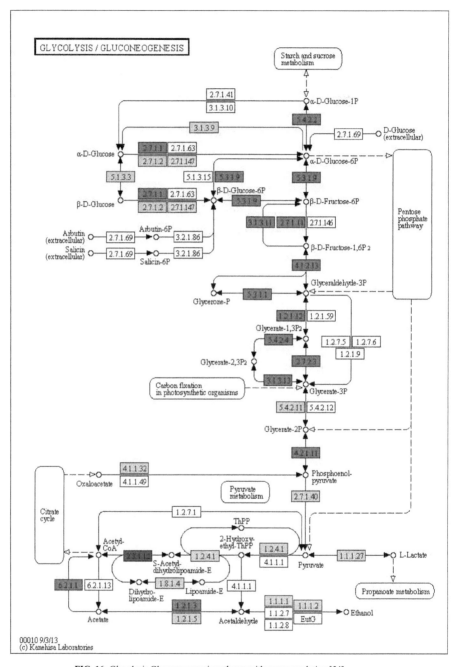

FIG. 16: Glycolysis Gluconeogenesis pathway with genes regulation [54].

From literature survey, it is obvious that sepsis increases glucose utilization which could be measured by lactate and alanine production. However, the increased glucose uptake is not accompanied by corresponding increase in glucose oxidation. Instead, the glucose carbon is released from peripheral tissues into the venous blood as lactate and alanine production are normal or increased, it appears that glucose uptake and glycolysis is accelerated in Sepsis. Thus, glucose carbon is conserved by the body because oxidation would deplete the body stores of glucose carbon. Highly upregulated transcripts in glycolysis pathway include HK3 (Hexokinases) which has high affinity for glucose and phosphorylate glucose to produce glucose-6-phosphate, which is the very first step in most glucose metabolism pathways [55].

4.5.3   Ribosome

Ribosomes are the cellular factories responsible for making proteins. In eukaryotes, ribosome biogenesis involves the production and correct assembly of four rRNAs and about 80 ribosomal proteins. It requires hundreds of factors not present in the mature particle. In the absence of these proteins, ribosome biogenesis is stalled and cell growth is terminated even under optimal growth conditions [56]. Down-regulation of ribosomal pathway states that there are no more protein formation in the patients that is the cells are not dividing.

In addition to transcriptional regulation, posttranscriptional modifications such as mRNA stabilization may lead to cytokine superinduction via ribosomal inactivation in leukocytes and gut epithelial cells. RPS24, RPL31, RPL13, RPL22L1, RPL5, RPS27A, RPL4, RPL15, RPL14 and RPL22 transcripts were among the top down-regulated genes in the Ribosomal pathway, and only RPL8 and RPL10 were up-regulated.

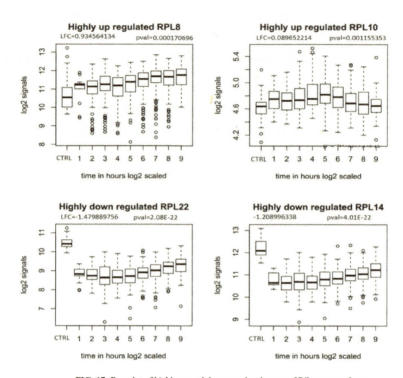

FIG. 17: Box plot of highly up and down regulated genes of Ribosome pathway

Results

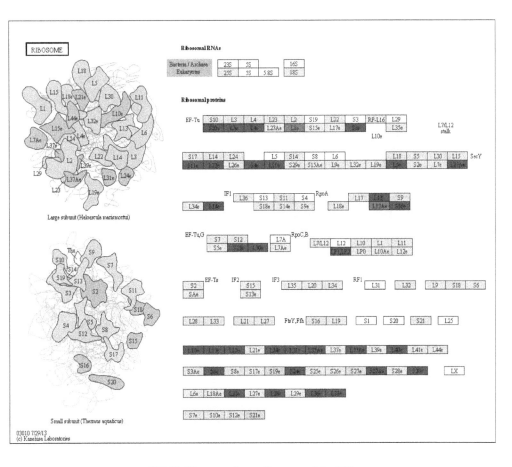

FIG. 18: Ribosome pathway with genes regulation [57].

4.6 Toll Like Receptors Signaling Pathway and Heatmap

TLR are the specific families of pattern recognition receptors that are responsible for detecting microbial pathogens and generating innate immune responses. Toll-like receptors (TLRs) are membrane-bound receptors identified as homologs of Toll in Drosophila. TLR signaling pathways are separated into two groups: a MyD88-dependent pathway that leads to the production of pro-inflammatory cytokines with quick activation

Results

of NF-{kappa}B and MAPK, and a MyD88-independent pathway associated with the induction of IFN-beta and IFN-inducible genes, and maturation of dendritic cells with slow activation of NF-{kappa}B and MAPK [58].

FIG. 19: TLR signalling pathway with genes regulation [59]

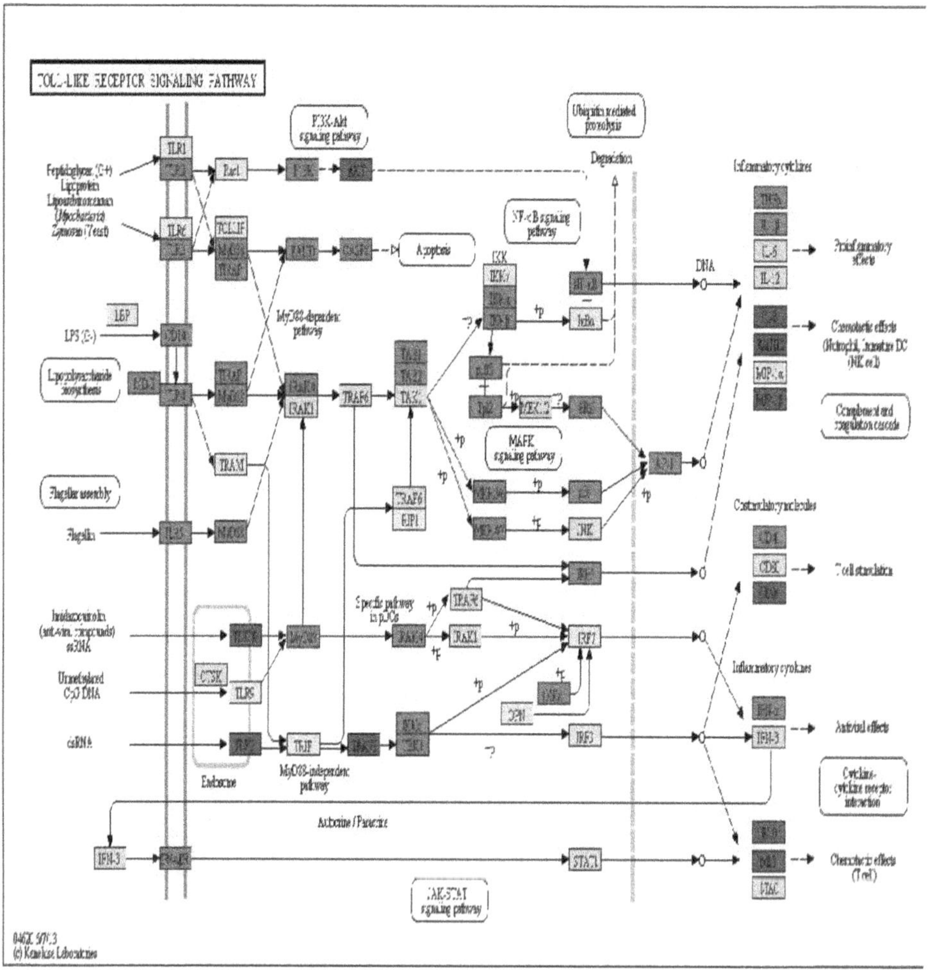

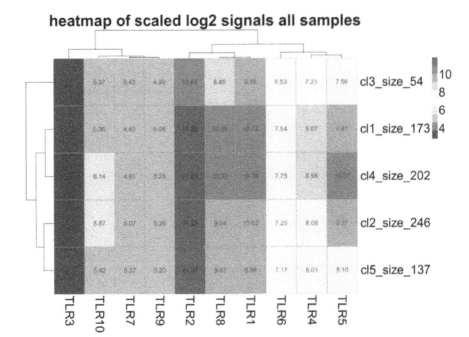

FIG. 20: TLR genes heatmap.

The expression of all of the Toll-like receptor (TLR) genes with the exception of TLR3, TLR 7 and TLR9, were increased after injury.

5. DISCUSSIONS

High-throughput transcriptomic data enable researchers to monitor molecular dynamics on a broad scale and to determine promising diagnostic as well as interventional targets. A more comprehensive characterisation of the genomic response to trauma is therefore required in order to increase our understanding of the molecular basis of clinical outcomes, leading to improvements in diagnosis and treatment.

The enrichment analysis offered several pathways, which seemed to be differentially expressed. The first one I choose is Glycolysis, as of its specificity for sepsis. It is obvious that this pathway is enriched in Septic patients, as the rate of body metabolism increases during the disease and body works more rapidly to provide energy to the cells. This is evidence that the results of the enrichment analysis are constructive. Precisely, glycolysis is commonly known to be the most important energy source for cells. So this pathway could reveal disparities between the metabolism in patients and in healthy controls. The second selected pathway is Ribosome pathway. This could be an interesting pathway.

I got the clinical data available from The Glue grant database (https://www.gluegrant.org/). The website had them and lots of more files about a year ago. Integrating the clinical variables give us more specific information regarding the conditions of a patient. Obviously, I found a very good correlation of IL5RA transcript with the Eosinophils (r > 0.6), so IL5RA could be a future biomarker. It is also possible to get the sample blood data, and perform some clinical tests and then incorporate the results with this data, possible, but not feasible (the clinicians don't like this associations for several reasons (e.g. after a long history of gene expression publications without this).

I found some outliers in the sex linked genes. Outliers relate also to controls and hint towards some wrongly mapped samples, but in overall there is above 99% correct mapping, so close to perfect. If it would be more, than one could expect trauma kicking up a gonosomal change, it isn't.

Just to reconfirm the activity of some genes during the Sepsis, I analyzed one more dataset. Total RNA extracted from whole blood (lysed in Tempus tubes) drawn from pediatric patients with acute community-acquired Staphylococcus aureus infection. This data contains the expression level of few genes (http://www.ncbi.nlm.nih.gov/geo/query/acc.cgi?acc=GSE30119). The main purpose to analyze this data is to evaluate the transcripts regulation during the Sepsis. It was very interesting that the LCN2 transcript was highly up regulated and the HLA-DMB was highly down regulated,

Discussions

confirming the transcripts regulation in Genomic Storm data.

The DEG numbers which I get were very high and these numbers could have been the result of False Positives, as the number of control samples was very few. So, I tried to compare the samples of first 24 samples and last 50 samples. Unfortunately, the no. of DEGs was still nearly the same in number.

I tried to develop the Models (with the linear modelling approach) for multiple effects gene-wise and the conclusion out of it was that, patient ID, so individual response seems to be more influential than time. While evaluating the single patient effects (by paired test), there were also some great results, for example, TXNIP (a gene responsible for type-1 and type-2 diabetes, pathway unknown) was found to be up regulated in older female. I believe that grouping the patients with of same age group and gender, could reveal many things.

REFERENCES:

[1] Mark Reimers, NCI,"An (opnionated) Guide to Microarray Data Aanalysis".

[2] http://www.people.vcu.edu/~mreimers/OGMDA/selecting.genes.html

[3] Jarno Tuimala, M. Minna Laine, DNA Microarray Data Analysis, CSC, Finnish Centre for Science; ISBN 952-9821-89-1; http://www.csc.fi/oppaat/siru/.

[4] Enuka Shay, 2003; Microarray cluster analysis and applications; University of Haifa.

[5] Angus DC, Linde-Zwirble WT, Lidicker J, Clermont G, Carcillo J, Pinsky MR: Epidemiology of severe sepsis in the United States: analysis of incidence, outcome and associated costs of care. Crit Care Med 2001, 29:1303-1310.

[6] Martin GS, Mennino DM, Eaton S, Moss M: The epidemiology of sepsis in the United States from 1979 through 2000. N Engl J Med 2003, 348:1546-1554.

[7] Alberti C, Brun-Buisson C, Burchardi H, Martin C, Goodman S, Artigas A, Sicignano A, Palazzo M, Moreno R, Boulmé R, Lepage E, et al.: Epidemiology of sepsis and infection in ICU patients from an international multicentre cohort study.

[8] http://www.cscc.uniklinikum-jena.de/en/Sepsis.html

[9] http://www.ccmtutorials.com/infection/sepsis/page3.htm

[10] American College of Chest Physicians/Society of Critical Care Medicine Consensus Conference: definitions for sepsis and organ failure and guidelines for the use of innovative therapies in sepsis. Crit Care Med 1992; 20(6):864-874.

[11] Bone, R.C., Balk, R.A., Cerra, F.B., Dellinger,R.P.., Fein, A.M., Knaus, W.A., et al. (1992). Definitions for sepsis and organ failure and guidelines for the use of innovative therapies in sepsis. The ACCP/SCCM Concensus Conference Committee. American College of Chest Physicians/society of Critical Care Medicine. Chest, 101, 1644-1655.

[12] DeCamp MM, Demling RH (1988) Posttraumatic multisystem organ failure. J Am Med Assoc 260: 530�34.

[13] Marshall JC, Vincent JL, Sibbald WJ (1995) Clinical Trials for the Treatment of Sepsis. Vincent JL, Sibbald WJ, eds. Berlin: Springer-Verlag. pp 122–138.

[14] Dewar D, Moore FA, Moore EE, Balogh Z (2009) Postinjury multiple organ failure. Injury 40: 912–918.

[15] Sasser, S.M., M. Varghese, M. Joshipura, and A. Kellermann. 2006. Preventing death and disability through the timely provision of pre-hospital trauma care. Bull. World Health Organ. 84:507. http://dx.doi.org/10.2471/BLT.06.033605.

References

[16] Probst, C., H.C. Pape, F. Hildebrand, G. Regel, L. Mahlke, P. Giannoudis, C. Krettek, and M.R. Grotz. 2009. 30 years of polytrauma care: An analysis of the change in strategies and results of 4849 cases treated at a single institution. Injury. 40:77–83. http://dx.doi.org/10.1016/ j.injury.2008.10.004.

[17] Lindig S, et al. Age-independent co-expression of antimicrobial gene clusters in the blood of septic patients. Int J Antimicrob Agents (2013), http://dx.doi.org/10.1016/j.ijantimicag.2013.04.012.

[18] Opal SM (2003) Clinical trial design and outcomes in patients with severe sepsis. Shock 20: 295–302.

[19] Baue AE (1997) Multiple organ failure, multiple organ dysfunction syndrome, and systemic inflammatory response syndrome. Why no magic bullets? Arch Surg 132: 703–707.

[20] Giannoudis, P.V. 2003. Current concepts of the inflammatory response after major trauma: An update. Injury. 34:397–404. http://dx.doi .org/10.1016/S0020-1383(02)00416-3

[21] DeLong, W.G. Jr., and C.T. Born. 2004. Cytokines in patients with poly- trauma. Clin. Orthop. Relat. Res. (422):57–65. http://dx.doi.org/10.1097/ 01.blo.0000130840.64528.1e

[22] Giannoudis, P.V., F. Hildebrand, and H.C. Pape. 2004. Inflammatory serum markers in patients with multiple trauma. Can they predict outcome? J. Bone Joint Surg. Br. 86:313–323. http://dx.doi.org/10.1302/0301-620X.86B3.15035

[23] Hotchkiss, R.S., A. Strasser, J.E. McDunn, and P.E. Swanson. 2009. Cell death. N. Engl. J. Med. 361:1570–1583. http://dx.doi.org/10.1056/NEJMra0901217

[24] Hotchkiss, R.S., and I.E. Karl. 2003. The pathophysiology and treatment of sepsis. N. Engl. J. Med. 348:138–150. http://dx.doi.org/10.1056/NEJMra021333

[25] Keel, M., and O. Trentz. 2005. Pathophysiology of polytrauma. Injury. 36:691–709. http://dx.doi.org/10.1016/j.injury.2004.12.037

[26] http://www.scmm.utmb.edu/genomics/microarrays/results.asp

[27] http://www.ncbi.nlm.nih.gov/geo/

[28] http://en.wikipedia.org/wiki/KEGG

[29] Kanehisa M (1997). "A database for post-genome analysis". Trends Genet 13 (9): 375–6. doi:10.1016/S0168-9525(97)01223-7. PMID 9287494

[30] Kanehisa M, Goto S, Hattori M, Aoki-Kinoshita KF, Itoh M, Kawashima S, et al. (2006). "From genomics to chemical genomics: new developments in KEGG". Nucleic Acids Res 34 (Database issue): D354–7. doi:10.1093/nar/gkj102. PMC 1347464. PMID 16381885.

[31] Xiao W, Mindrinos MN, Seok J, Cuschieri J et al. A genomic storm in critically injured humans. J Exp Med 2011 Dec 19;208(13):2581-90. PMID: 22110166

References

[32] Gentleman RC, Carey VJ, Bates DM, Bolstad B, Dettling M, Dudoit S, et al. Bioconductor: open software development for computational biology and bioinformatics. Genome Biol 2004;5:R80.

[33] Xiao W, Mindrinos MN, Seok J, Cuschieri J et al. A genomic storm in critically injured humans. J Exp Med 2011 Dec 19;208(13):2581-90. PMID: 22110166

[34] Sandberg R, Larsson O. Improved precision and accuracy for microarrays using updated probe set definitions. BMC Bioinformatics 2007;8:48.

[35] Shi L, Jones WD, Jensen RV, Harris SC, Perkins RG, Goodsaid FM, et al. The balance of reproducibility, sensitivity, and specificity of lists of differentially expressed genes in microarray studies. BMC Bioinformatics 2008;9(Suppl. 9):S10.

[36] Paradis E., Claude J. & Strimmer K. 2004. APE: analyses of phylogenetics and evolution in R language. Bioinformatics 20: 289-290.

[37] Yaari G, Bolen CR, Thakar J, Kleinstein SH. Quantitative set analysis for gene expression: a method to quantify gene set differential expression including gene-gene correlations. Nucleic Acids Res. 2013 Aug 5.

[38] A Basis for Brain and Adaptive Systems, by Zhe Chen, Simon Haykin, Jos J. Eggermont, and Suzanna Becker Copyright☐2007 John Wiley & Sons, Inc.

[39] http://en.wikipedia.org/wiki/HLA-DMB

[40] http://www.lifetechnologies.com/in/en/home/life-science/cell-analysis/signaling-pathways/t-cell-receptor-tcr/t-cell-receptor-tcr-overview.html

[41] http://www.genome.jp/kegg-bin/show_pathway?hsa04612

[42] Kjeldsen L, Johnsen AH, Sengeløv H, Borregaard N (May 1993). "Isolation and primary structure of NGAL, a novel protein associated with human neutrophil gelatinase". J. Biol. Chem. 268 (14): 10425–32. PMID 7683678

[43] Nelson AM, Zhao W, Gilliland KL, Zaenglein AL, Liu W, Thiboutot DM (April 2008). "Neutrophil gelatinase–associated lipocalin mediates 13-cis retinoic acid–induced apoptosis of human sebaceous gland cells". J. Clin. Invest. 118 (4): 1468–78. doi:10.1172/JCI33869. PMC 2262030. PMID 18317594

[44] Nelson AM, Zhao W, Gilliland KL, Zaenglein AL, Liu W, Thiboutot DM (March/April 2009). "Early gene changes induced by isotretinoin in the skin provide clues to its mechanism of action". Dermato-Endocrinology 1 (2): 100–1. doi:10.4161/derm.1.2.8107. PMC 2835899. PMID 20224692.

[45] Sánchez L, Calvo M, Brock JH (1992). "Biological role of lactoferrin". Arch. Dis. Child. 67 (5): 657–61. doi:10.1136/adc.67.5.657. PMC 1793702. PMID 1599309.

References

[46] Rogan MP, Geraghty P, Greene CM, O'Neill SJ, Taggart CC, McElvaney NG (2006). "Antimicrobial proteins and polypeptides in pulmonary innate defence". Respir. Res. 7 (1): 29. doi:10.1186/1465-9921-7-29. PMC 1386663. PMID 16503962

[47] http://www.ncbi.nlm.nih.gov/gene/6521

[48] http://www.uniprot.org/uniprot/P02730

[49] http://www.ncbi.nlm.nih.gov/gene?cmd=Retrieve&dopt=full_report&list_uids=3568

[50] Nurko, Samuel; Furuta, G T (2006). "Eosinophilic esophagitis". GI Motility online. doi:10.1038/gimo49

[51] Lahn BT, Page DC (Nov 1997). "Functional coherence of the human Y chromosome". Science 278 (5338): 675–80. doi:10.1126/science.278.5338.675. PMID 9381176.

[52] "Entrez Gene: DDX3Y DEAD (Asp-Glu-Ala-Asp) box polypeptide 3, Y-linked".

[53] http://www.genome.jp/dbget-bin/www_bget?pathway+hsa00010

[54] http://www.genome.jp/kegg-bin/show_pathway?13906663561694/hsa00010.args

[55] http://web.squ.edu.om/med-Lib/MED_CD/E_CDs/anesthesia/site/content/v05/050132r00.HTM

[56] http://www.genome.jp/dbget-bin/www_bget?hsa03008

[57] http://www.genome.jp/kegg-bin/show_pathway?map=ko03010&show_description=show

[58] http://www.wikipathways.org/index.php/Pathway:WP75

[59] http://www.genome.jp/kegg-bin/show_pathway?139072973331064/hsa04620.args

Pathogen Escherichia Coli Infection (hsa05130)

Enteropathogenic E. coli (EPEC) and enterohemorrhagic E. coli (EHEC) are closely related pathogenic strains of Escherichia coli. The hallmark of EPEC/EHEC infections [DS:H00278 H00277] is induction of attaching and effacing (A/E) lesions that damage intestinal epithelial cells. The capacity to form A/E lesions is encoded mainly by the locus of enterocyte effacement (LEE) pathogenicity island. Tir, Map, EspF, EspG are known LEE-encoded effector proteins secreted via the type III secretion system, which is also LEE-encoded, into the host cell. EPEC and EHEC Tir's link the extracellular bacterium to the cell cytoskeleton. Map and EspF are involved in mitochondrion membrane permeabilization. EspG interacts with tubulins and stimulates microtubule destabilization. LEE-encoded adhesin or intimin (Eae) is exported via the general secretory pathway to the periplasm, where it is inserted into the outer membrane. In addition to Tir, two potential host cell-carried intimin receptors, beta1 integrin (ITGB1) and nucleolin (NCL), have so far been identified. The distinguishing feature of EHEC is the elaboration of Shiga-like toxin (Stx). Stx cleaves ribosomal RNA, thereby disrupting protein synthesis and killing the intoxicated epithelial or endothelial cells.

Ref: http://www.genome.jp/dbget-bin/www_bget?pathway+hsa05130

Supplementary

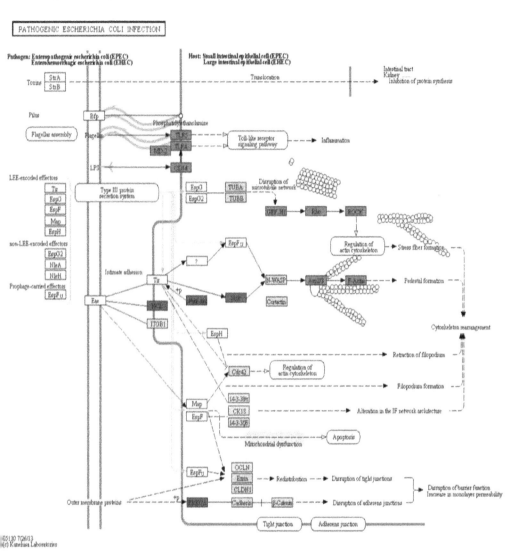

FIG. 21: Pathogen Escherichia Coli Infection (hsa05130)

Ref: http://www.genome.jp/kegg-bin/show_pathway?139066444614146/hsa05130.args

Supplementary

Aminocyl tRNA Biosynthesis (hsa00970)

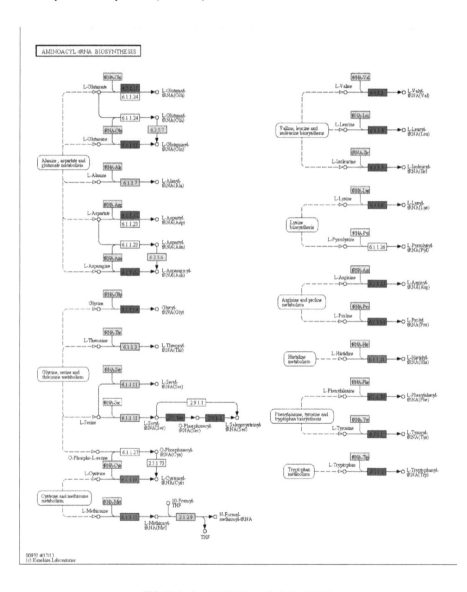

FIG. 22: Aminocyl tRNA Biosynthesis (hsa00970)

Ref: http://www.genome.jp/kegg-bin/show_pathway?13906679097745/hsa00970.args

Supplementary

Galactose Metabolism (hsa00052)

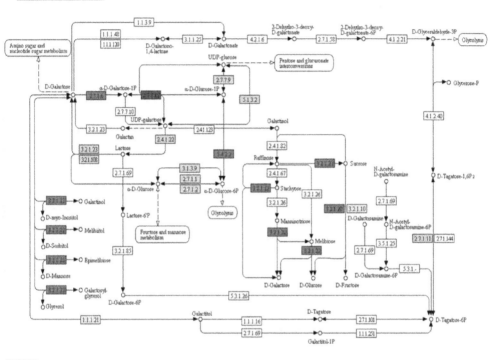

FIG. 23: Galactose Metabolism (hsa00052)

Ref: http://www.genome.jp/kegg-bin/show_pathway?hsa00052